Table of Contents

The Need for Speed

Cheetahs are the world's fastest land animals. In just seconds, they can reach speeds up to 70 miles (113 kilometers) per hour. That is as fast as a car travels on the highway! But these cats use their energy quickly. They can sprint only for short bursts.

A cheetah's stretchy spine helps the animal take long strides.

Built for Speed

Lisa M. Herrington

Content Consultant
Carrie Pratt
Curator, North America Region
Columbus Zoo and Aquarium, Columbus, Ohio

Reading Consultant
Jeanne M. Clidas, Ph.D.
Reading Specialist

Children's Press®
An Imprint of Scholastic Inc.

Library of Congress Cataloging-in-Publication Data

Names: Herrington, Lisa M., author.

Title: Built for speed: Kangaroos! Cheetahs! Lizards!/by Lisa M. Herrington.

Description: New York, NY: Children's Press, an imprint of Scholastic Inc., 2019. | Series: Rookie STAR. Extraordinary animals | Includes index.

Identifiers: LCCN 2017025798| ISBN 9780531230893 (library binding) |

ISBN 9780531233788 (pbk.)

Subjects: LCSH: Animal locomotion—Juvenile literature. | Animals—Adaptations Juvenile literature. | Speed—Juvenile literature.

Classification: LCC QP301.H39 2018 | DDC 591.5/7—dc23

LC record available at https://lccn.loc.gov/2017025798

Produced by Spooky Cheetah Press
Art direction: Keith Plechaty for kwpCreative
Creative direction: Judith Christ-Lafond for Scholastic

© 2019 by Scholastic Inc. All rights reserved.

Published in 2019 by Children's Press, an imprint of Scholastic Inc.

Printed in Johor Bahru, Malaysia 108

SCHOLASTIC, CHILDREN'S PRESS, ROOKIE STAR™, and associated logos are trademarks and/or registered trademarks of Scholastic Inc.

1 2 3 4 5 6 7 8 9 10 R 28 27 26 25 24 23 22 21 20 19

Scholastic Inc., 557 Broadway, New York, NY 10012.

Photographs ©:cover: Bence Mate/Minden Pictures; 1: Ron Reznick/VW Pics/UIG/Getty Images; 2: fivespots/Shutterstock; 3: FLPA/Superstock, Inc.; 4-5: Kandfoto/Getty Images; 6-7: Bence Mate/Minden Pictures; 8 inset: landbysea/iStockphoto; 8-9: mallardg500/Getty Images; 10-11: Huw Cordey/NPL/Minden Pictures; 10 center: Barry Mansell/Nature Picture Library; 11 inset: Merlin Tuttle/Science Source; 12-13: Solvin Zankl/Nature Picture Library; 13 inset: Ralph Lee Hopkins/Media Bakery; 14-15: Martin Strmiska/Alamy Images; 15 inset: NaturePL/Superstock, Inc.; 16-17: FLPA/Superstock, Inc.; 17 inset: FLPA/Superstock, Inc.; 18 inset: picturepartners/Shutterstock; 18-19: Klein & Hubert/Nature Picture Library; 19 inset: dpa picture alliance/Alamy Images; 20-21: Ron Reznick/VW Pics/UIG/Getty Images; 21 sidebarinset: bobloblaw/Getty Images; 22-23: Minden Pictures/Superstock, Inc.; 23 inset: Satoshi Kuribayashi/Nature Production/Minden Pictures; 24-25: Kim Taylor/NPL/Minden Pictures; 25 inset: Jack Milchanowski/Getty Images; 26-27: Thomas P. Peschak/Getty Images; 27 inset: David Doubilet/National Geographic Creative; 28 top: Visuals Unlimited, Inc./Ken Catania/Getty Images; 28 -29 ribbons: _human/iStockphoto; 29 top: Mary ClayPantheo/Pantheon/Superstock, Inc.; 30 top: LUNAMARINA/Thinkstock; 30 center top: JohnCarnemolla/iStockphoto; 30 center: Sam Hobson/Nature Picture Library; 30 center bottom: Stephen J Krasemann/Getty Images; 30 bottom: zokru/iStockphoto; 31 top: Thomas P. Peschak/Getty Images; 31 bottom: David Doubilet/National Geographic Creative; 31 center bottom: Martin Strmiska/Alamy Images; 31 center top: landbysea/iStockphoto; 32: Hiroya Minakuchi/Minden Pictures/Superstock, Inc.

Many animals are super speedy. Being fast helps them survive. **Predators** have to chase down other animals for food. **Prey** need to be fast to get away. Some animals are especially

The basilisk's light body and special feet help it sprint on water.

good at moving quickly. This basilisk lizard darts across the top of water to escape danger. Let's learn about other extraordinary animals that live in the fast lane.

Chapter 1

Fastest Fliers and Swimmers

Would you believe this bird flies faster than a train travels? The peregrine falcon can dive from above at more than 200 miles (322 kilometers) per hour. It is the fastest animal on Earth. The falcon swoops down and grabs other birds in midair with its sharp claws. The feast can begin!

Peregrines are built for speed. A sleek body shape and strong chest muscles help these birds dive fast. Light bones make them less heavy in the air. And pointed wings and stiff feathers power them downward.

A peregrine falcon uses its excellent eyesight to spot prey.

Scientists once thought birds were the fastest fliers. Then they tracked a mammal that can fly: the Brazilian free-tailed bat. This fantastic flier reaches speeds of up to 100 miles (161 kilometers) per hour. At night, millions of bats spiral out from their caves to hunt. They snatch thousands of insects right out of the sky.

Brazilian free-tailed bats swarm through the sky in large groups.

Brazilian free-tailed bats are tiny. They weigh about as much as three nickels. Their sleek bodies and long, narrow wings help the bats race through the air.

Gentoo penguins cannot fly through the air. But they can cruise through the icy ocean at 22 miles (35 kilometers) per hour. Gentoos are the fastest-swimming birds. Their smooth, sleek shape allows them to cut through the water. And their flippers act as paddles. These penguins dive as many as 450 times a day in search of their favorite prey—krill and fish.

A gentoo can hold its breath underwater for seven minutes.

Gentoos may not really fly, but they sure look like they do! When a gentoo is being chased by a predator, the penguin can jump out of the water for a quick escape. Gentoos move even faster through air than they do through water.

The sailfish is the world's fastest fish. It can swim at about 68 miles (109 kilometers) per hour. A sailfish's long bill and sleek body help it whisk through the water. It slices through the ocean to snatch supper. The sailfish eats smaller fish such as sardines and anchovies.

Can you guess how the sailfish gets its name? Its back fin looks like a giant sail. A sailfish uses its fin to round up smaller fish. Then it slashes through the group with its sharp, swordlike bill.

Chapter 2

Fastest Runners and Jumpers

Bounce, bounce, bounce! A red kangaroo leaves predators in the dust. It can reach speeds of 35 miles (56 kilometers) per hour. This animal makes huge jumps on its powerful back legs. In a single hop, it can leap nearly the length of a school bus!

At around eight months old, a baby kangaroo is ready to leave its mother's pouch and hop along behind her!

Hares are hurried hoppers, too. In fact, they have been clocked at speeds of up to 47 miles (76 kilometers) per hour. Like kangaroos, hares get their power from their strong, long hind legs.

Most birds fly away to escape danger. But ostriches—the world's tallest and heaviest birds—cannot fly. They are too big. Instead, they use their long, thin legs to speed across the African plains. They don't want to become a lion's dinner! At 43 miles (69 kilometers) per hour, ostriches are the fastest-running birds on Earth. They also lay the biggest eggs of any birds!

ostrich egg

Chicken egg

An ostrich can cover 16 feet (5 meters) in one stride!

Why do ostriches have wings if they cannot fly? These big birds open their wings like sails as they run. Their wings help them balance. Ostriches also use their wings to quickly change direction.

Pronghorn have big eyes to spot predators.

Meet the marathon runners of the animal world. Pronghorn are the fastest animals over long distances. They are also the fastest land animals in North America. Pronghorn can outrun hungry wolves and coyotes at speeds of 60 miles (97 kilometers) per hour.

The pronghorn is almost as fast as the cheetah. But a pronghorn can keep its swift pace going longer. Its strong hooves are cushioned for running far. Its extra-large lungs and heart provide lots of oxygen to the pronghorn's muscles.

Chapter 3

Fastest Attackers

This trap-jaw ant has the world's fastest bite. It can snap its mouth shut at a whopping speed of 145 miles (233 kilometers) per hour. That is 2,300 times as fast as you can blink your eye! For a quick getaway, the trap-jaw ant can jam its jaws at the ground and launch itself through the air.

A trap-jaw ant carries its prey in its jaws.

When it comes to speed, the bombardier beetle is also a champ. This insect can spray boiling-hot liquid at predators. It can fire the scalding spray at up to 22 miles (35 kilometers) per hour.

No other animal has a tongue faster than the chameleon's. This colorful lizard hunts insects in trees. A chameleon can snap its long tongue around a tasty insect at 13 miles (21 kilometers) per hour. Once the tongue's sticky tip lands on an insect, there is no escape. In less than a second, the chameleon pulls the prey into its mouth.

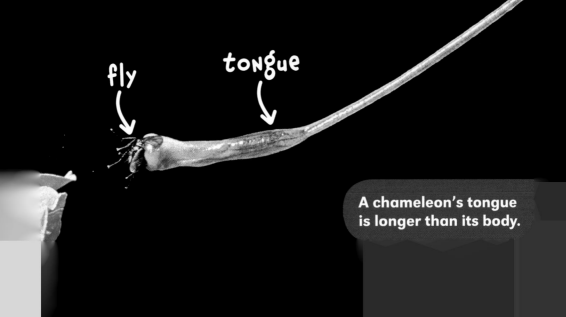

fly

tongue

A chameleon's tongue is longer than its body.

Chameleons have incredible eyes. They can rotate each eye individually. This lets the chameleon search for prey in every direction. After spotting an insect, this swift eater strikes with its fast-moving tongue!

eye

Don't let their name fool you. Jellyfish are not really fish. They are **invertebrates**. Those are animals without backbones. Jellyfish hunt shrimp and fish. They use **venom** in their tentacles to kill their prey. This stuns the prey before they eat it. Jellyfish have the fastest sting. It takes them just a fraction of a second to strike their target. Like the other creatures in this book, jellyfish have speed on their side.

To sting prey, a jellyfish uses tentacles that hang from its body.

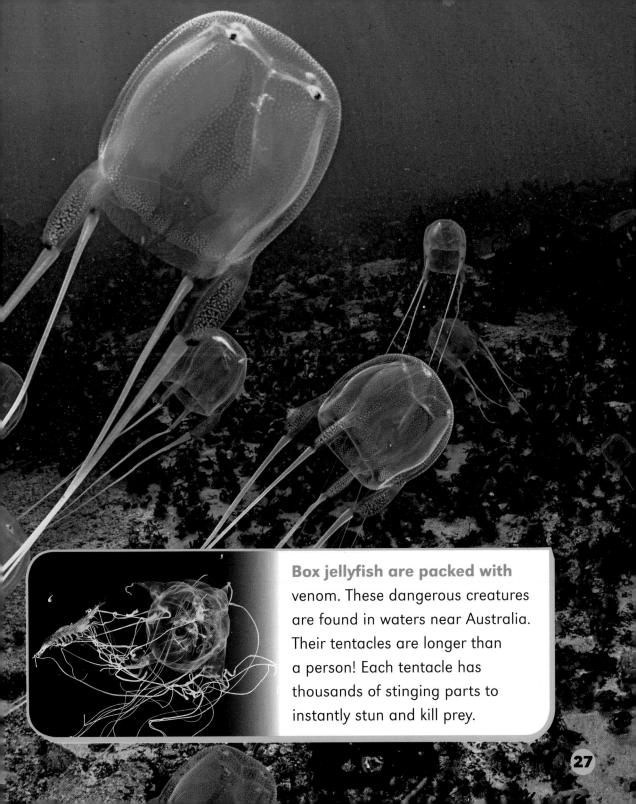

Box jellyfish are packed with venom. These dangerous creatures are found in waters near Australia. Their tentacles are longer than a person! Each tentacle has thousands of stinging parts to instantly stun and kill prey.

Which IS More Extraordinary?

Fastest-Eating Mammal

Star-Nosed Mole

- This odd-looking mole can chow down on an insect or earthworm in less than a second.

- The mole's nose is shaped like a star. It has 22 pink, fingerlike parts.

- The mole uses its nose to find worms, insects, and other prey.

You Decide!

Get to know two lightning-fast animals and make your own choice.

Aardvark

- In 15 seconds, an aardvark can dig a hole about 2 feet (1 meter) deep.

- An aardvark digs to find food, escape danger, and make underground holes to live in.

- Aardvarks use their long, sticky tongues to gobble up ants and termites.

Fastest-Digging Animal

The Race Is On!

Check out some animals that clock super speeds. Then answer the questions below.

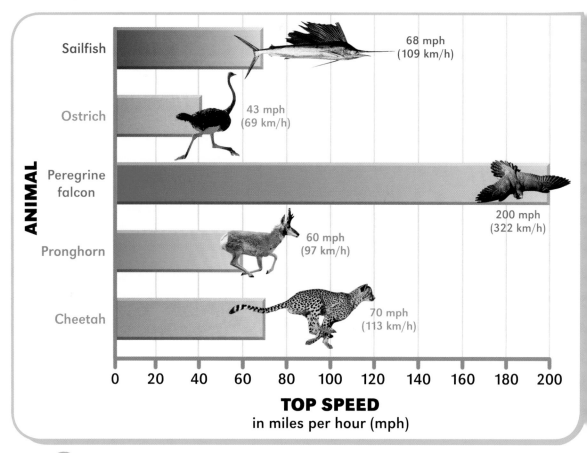

ANIMAL

- Sailfish — 68 mph (109 km/h)
- Ostrich — 43 mph (69 km/h)
- Peregrine falcon — 200 mph (322 km/h)
- Pronghorn — 60 mph (97 km/h)
- Cheetah — 70 mph (113 km/h)

TOP SPEED
in miles per hour (mph)

0   20   40   60   80   100   120   140   160   180   200

1 Which animal runs, flies, hops, or swims fastest?

2 How many animals can reach at least 60 mph?

3 Which two animals might have a race that ends in a tie?

ANSWERS: 1. peregrine falcon; 2. four; 3. cheetah and sailfish

Glossary

invertebrates (in-**vur**-tuh-brits): Animals without backbones.

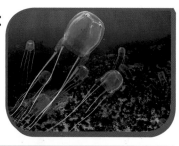

predators (**pred**-uh-turs): Animals that hunt other animals for food.

prey (**pray**): Animal that is hunted by another animal for food.

venom (**ven**-uhm): Poison produced by some snakes, spiders, and jellyfish.

Index

Facts for Now

Visit this Scholastic Web site for more information
on speedy animals:
www.factsfornow.scholastic.com
Enter the keywords **Built for Speed**

About the Author

Lisa M. Herrington has written many children's books about animals. She loves to learn fascinating facts about them. Lisa lives in Connecticut with her husband, Ryan, and daughter, Caroline.